"It is uplifting and encouraging to read and meditate on these inspirational poems and prayers. This book can serve as hope for those who may be hopeless—it can bring joy to those who are down and out...bring peace to those who are at war with themselves and others. It's truly an inspirational book."

Rev. Earnest Ray Taylor
Teacher, Writer, Author
Author: Overcoming the ODDS

"Such a work as this meets amply a definite need. There can be no question of the value of this book from many standpoints; it is a roadmap that one can follow to escape boredom, depression, and the many difficult challenges of life."

Fay Tacker-English teacher, 7th grade,
Lindale Junior High
Lindale, Texas

"Everyone can benefit from reading this book. The message gives hope and is timeless."

Karen Albright
Teacher

Restore The Joy

Restore The Joy

A Collection of Inspirational Poetry & Prayers

Poems by Doris M. Batson,
Prayers by Rev. P.R. Moore

iUniverse, Inc.
New York Lincoln Shanghai

Restore The Joy
A Collection of Inspirational Poetry & Prayers

Copyright © 2005 by Doris M. Batson

All rights reserved. No part of this book may be used or reproduced by any means, graphic, electronic, or mechanical, including photocopying, recording, taping or by any information storage retrieval system without the written permission of the publisher except in the case of brief quotations embodied in critical articles and reviews.

iUniverse books may be ordered through booksellers or by contacting:

iUniverse
2021 Pine Lake Road, Suite 100
Lincoln, NE 68512
www.iuniverse.com
1-800-Authors (1-800-288-4677)

Scripture quotations marked "KJV" are taken from the Holy Bible, King James Version, Thomas Nelson, Inc., Copyright© 1994.

Scriptures taken from the HOLY BIBLE, NEW INTERNATIONAL VERSION®. Copyright© 1973, 1978, 1984 by International Bible Society. Used by permission of Zondervan Publishing House. All rights reserved.

ISBN: 0-595-33903-4 (pbk)
ISBN: 0-595-67029-6 (cloth)

Printed in the United States of America

*This book is dedicated to my Heavenly Father,
the source of my Joy, Hope and Inspiration.
To my mother, father, and aunt who with every ounce of their
love, have been there to support the family in anyway they could,
and to those who have given words of encouragement and
listened patiently when I needed a listening ear…*

*Thank you,
for believing!*

To
_____

From
_____

Date
_____

Contents

Introduction .... *xv*

Chapter 1 Restoration 1
A Prayer of Restoration *3*
Restore the Joy *4*
One Rose *6*
Stitches *10*
Shoes *14*
Thirsty *18*

Chapter 2 Seeking God's Guidance 21
A Prayer for Guidance *23*
The Path *24*
Too Busy *29*
If I Could... .... *31*
Beatitudes Of a Christian Marriage *34*
Forgive Me *36*

Chapter 3 Proclaiming The Joy! 38
A Prayer Of Joyfulness *40*
I get Joy *41*
A Song Bird Chorus *44*
By The Window *47*
Colors of love *50*
Formula III *52*

Chapter 4 Deliverance	58
A Prayer of Deliverance	*60*
Be of Good Courage...	*61*
A Spider's Song	*63*
Why	*66*
Available	*69*
The Challenge	*71*
Symphony	*73*
Stand	*76*
The Divine Creator Awe ~Inspiring	*79*
Chapter 5 A Prayer For All Seasons	86
Prayer for Daily Guidance	*87*
Prayer for Dedication of Soul and Body	*87*
Prayer for Christian Service	*87*
Prayer for The Children	*88*
A General Prayer Of Thanksgiving	*88*
A Prayer for the Missions	*88*
A Prayer for Fruitful Seasons	*89*
A Prayer for Memorial Days	*89*
A Prayer for the Clergy and People	*89*
A Prayer for Those under affliction	*90*
A Prayer in time Of Famine	*90*
A Prayer for Families	*90*
Personal Prayer	91
Inspirational Quote	*92*
About the Authors	*93*

Acknowledgements

It has always been inspiring through the years, observing my father as he would plan and prepare his weekly sermons. The enthusiasm of watching him contemplate and challenge his ideas was in itself an humbling experience. Of course, in retrospect, it was seeing his drive and determination that encouraged me to continue reaching and challenging my dreams and ideas as well.

In co-writing this book with my father, it has been a fulfilling journey…one that has given us both an opportunity to experience an inspirational blessing and sense of inner fulfillment in being able to write and create this book.

So to my father…I say thank you for the insight and inspirational words of encouragement to "never give up on a dream". To my sister, Fayetta Taylor and daughter, Brittany Batson,…thank you for sharing your love and continued support. I dare not conclude without giving thanks to my feisty yet God-fearing mother who has always instilled in all her children the wisdom to know, that no matter what life's challenges may bring…God is always in control…always watching…always protecting, and will never let you down. She is a solid rock, and has always been an inspiration.

A special thanks to my co-workers: Carolyn Westbrook, Karen Albright, Fay Tacker, Pam Slaughter, John Aaron and all who were there to listen, and offer encouraging words. Truly, it is a blessing to have the support of wonderful friends and family. Thanks to all of you.

Introduction

My brethren, count it all joy when ye fall into divers temptations; knowing this that the trying of your faith worketh patience. But let patience have her perfect work, that ye may be perfect and entire, wanting nothing.

—James 1:2-6

Joy, a gift of hope…one in which the promises of God are poured into our spirit of belief that no matter what situation or challenge may arise in our lives from day to day; there is hope in knowing that the struggles of life may be overcome in realizing, God is always with us…right by our side and will always give us strength to endure.

The preface of this book underscores the theme of restoration and the willingness to keep the faith even through life's trials and tribulations. We are reminded in Psalm 30:5 that "weeping may endure for a night, but joy cometh in the morning." Even though we may sometimes become discouraged and disheartened, we can still rely upon the promises of God, in knowing he will guide and sustain us to overcome and confront whatever life's challenges may come our way.

This book is divided into five chapters. Chapter one focuses upon the inner desire to discover a renewal of the spirit and to find inner strength and fulfillment of God's abiding love within. Chapter two, thereafter, provides insight into the importance and willingness to follow in his footsteps, so as to avoid pitfalls and unexpected obstacles that may venture into our pathway . If we become determined to seek and live according to His will, we can undoubtedly as Chapter three points out…Proclaim the Joy, and experience the wonderful discovery of praise, in rejoicing and praising His Holy Name.

Chapter Four entitled Strength and Deliverance, focuses upon providing encouraging words of comfort and the affirmation of faith…being ever mindful that whatever our needs, desires, hopes or aspirations; God will provide. Matthew 6:33 states: "But seek ye first the kingdom of God, and his righteousness; and all these things shall be added unto you". If we seek him first and stand firm on our beliefs, we can believe with profound assurance that there are no boundaries with God, and remember, as Mark 10:27 states: "With men it is impossible, but not with God; for with God all things are possible."

The final chapter of the book concludes with inspirational prayers whose devotional messages will prayerfully enrich and strengthen those seeking spiritual guidance and growth.

It is our prayer that each scripture, prayer and poem of this book will offer words of encouragement, and will be an inspirational blessing to all who may be aspiring to discover the fulfillment and contentment of His Love and Joy.

1

Restoration

"Renew a Right Spirit in me"

Create in Me a Clean Heart, O God,
and renew a right spirit in me.
Psalm 51:10 KJV

A Prayer of Restoration

Lord, I ask You to restore unto me the Joy of Your salvation. Where there is pain, restore it with the comfort of peace. Where there is sorrow, restore it with the perseverance of Your healing grace. When it seems like there is no hope, give me renewed wisdom to know that no matter what obstacles may come my way, You will provide strength and courage to help me make it through. Create in me a clean heart oh Lord and renew in me a right spirit. Shine on me the Light of Your Salvation and help me to abound always in the love of Your Amazing Grace.

Amen

Restore the Joy

Restore the Joy of Your salvation Lord
This is my humble plea

Cleanse my heart and my soul
Renew a right spirit in me

Restore the Joy of Your salvation Lord
For when my heart is filled with sorrow

Be my comforter and my strength
My Joy and hope for tomorrow

Restore the Joy of Your salvation Lord
My Life, My Body, My Soul and Mind

Dwell as a beacon within me
Let Your light forever shine

Restore the Joy of Your salvation Lord
I am leaning and depending on You

To help me run this Christian race
Lead and guide me safely through

Restore the Joy of Your salvation Lord
I submit myself humbly to thee

For I am Yours…Completely
Take Me…Shape Me…
Restore Me…

This is My Humble Plea!

Restore the Joy

Psalm 51:12
Restore unto me the joy of thy salvation; and uphold me with thy free spirit.

Psalm 23:3
He restoreth my soul: he leadeth me in the paths of righteousness for his name's sake.

2 Corinthians 5:17
Therefore if any man be in Christ, he is a new creature: old things are passed away; behold, all things are become new.

Romans 12:2
And be not, conformed to this world: but be ye transformed by the renewing of your mind, that ye may prove what is that good, and acceptable, and perfect, will of God.

Psalm 46:1
God is our refuge and strength, a very present help in trouble.

Matthew 5:6 NIV
Blessed are those who hunger and thirst for righteousness; for they will be filled.

Psalm 80:19NIV
Restore us, O Lord God Almighty; make your face shine upon us, that we may be saved.

One Rose

One Loving
One Rose

One Beauty
One Rose

One Everlasting
One Rose

One Pure
One Rose

One Saviour
One Rose

One Bleeding
One Rose

One Forgiving
One Rose

One Seed
One Rose

One Gift
One Rose

One Color
One Rose

One Skin
One Rose

One Shining
One Rose

One Enduring
One Rose

One Giving
One Rose

One Caring
One Rose

One Sharing
One Rose

One Faithful
One Rose

One Hope
One Rose

One Love
One Rose

One Peace
One Rose

One Joy
One Rose

Within
One Rose

One Rose

Nehemiah 8:10
For the Joy of the Lord is your strength.

Isaiah 60:1
Arise, shine, for thy light is come, and the Lord is risen upon thee.

Lamentations 3:23
They are new every morning: great is thy faithfulness.

Philippians 4:8
Finally, brethren, whatsoever things are true, whatsoever things are honest, whatsoever things are just, whatsoever things are pure, whatsoever things are lovely, whatsoever things are of good report; If there be any virtue, and if there be any praise, think on these things.

Ephesians 2:14
For he is our peace, who hath made both one, and hath broken down the middle wall of partition between us.

Isaiah 60:19
The sun shall be no more thy light by day; neither for brightness shall the moon give light unto thee; but the Lord shall be unto thee an everlasting light, and thy God thy glory.

John 15:13
Greater love hath no man than this, that a man lay down his life for his friends.

I Timothy 4:10
For therefore we both labour and suffer reproach, because we trust in the living God, who is the saviour of all men, specially of those that believe.

I Peter 5:7
Casting all your care upon him; for he careth for you.

John 14:27
Peace I leave with you, my peace I give unto you: not as the world giveth, give I unto you. Let not your heart be troubled, neither let it be afraid.

Stitches

An old battered and
Fragile worn out rag
Torn apart by years
Of life's trials and tribulations

Fibers unkept and shredded
Ends warn and raveled
Desperate need
Of restoration

Once finely kept
Colors pure and bright
Every stitch
Strong and bold

A broken stitch…
Now break the threads
Of one garment
Once made whole

Soiled stains
Cover
Loosely unwoven
Knit grains

Each deteriorating wash
Break chains of stitches
Over and over
Again

A weathered garment
Once new

Now broken down
In despair

Only one can save
Only one can restore
Only one
Can heal and repair

One stitch at a time
He can weave each thread
Give it a brand
New direction

One stitch at a time
He can take a weathered
Garment and
Restore its imperfections

One stitch at a time
He can revitalize, energize
Woven fibers from
End to end

One stitch at a time
New luster, New shine
Can be restored
Once again

One stitch at a time
He can repair…revive
And offer
Restoration

One stitch at a time
He can re-shape,
Each stitch completely

Make it a new
Creation…

God's love is intertwined
Within us
The fibers of our soul

One stitch at a time
His love can wash us
Cleanse our guilty stains

And once again
Re-new us re-store us
And make us completely
Whole

Stitches

Ephesians 4:23-24
And be renewed in the spirit of your mind; and that ye put on the new man, which after God is created in righteousness and true holiness.

2 Corinthians 5:17
Therefore, if any man be in Christ, he is a new creation; old things are passed away; behold, all things are become new.

Romans 5:3-4
And not only so, but we glory in tribulation's also, knowing that tribulation; worketh patience; and patience, experience, and experience hope.

John 16:33
These things I have spoken unto you that in me ye might have peace. In the world ye shall have tribulation: but be of good cheer; I have overcome the world.

Psalm 139:13-14NIV
For you created my inmost being; you knit me together in my mother's womb. I praise you because I am fearfully and wonderfully made; your works are wonderful, I know that full well.

Shoes

*Beat down
Battered
Worn Out
Run Down
Buckled up
Laced, Tied and
Tangled up...*

*But...
My Soul is Happy Running
For the Lord*

*Washed Out
Faded
Crinkled
Wrinkled
Stepped In
Stepped On
Trampled On Every Side*

*But...
My Soul is Happy Running
For the Lord*

*Zipped,
Ripped,
Tarnished
Unpolished
Used
Misused and Abused*

But…
My Soul is Happy
Running For the Lord

Heel Warn
Needs Repair
Scuff Marks
Linger From
Wear and Tear
Kicked, Tossed
Pushed and
Shuffled Around

But…
My Soul is Happy
Running For The Lord…

This abuse is small
Seems like almost
Nothing at all

Compared to what
He did for me

He rescued,
Salvaged and
Saved my soul

And now I am
debt Free

My Soul is Happy
Running For the Lord…

And I'm Not Tired Yet!!!

Shoes

1 Corinthians 9:2-4
Know ye not that they who run in a race run all, but one receiveth the prize. So run, that ye may obtain.

Hebrews 12:1-2
Wherefore, seeing we also are compassed about with so great a cloud of witnesses, let us lay aside every weight, and the sin which doth so easily beset us, and let us run with patience the race that is set before us. Looking unto Jesus, the author and finisher of our faith, who for the joy that was set before him endured the cross, despising the shame, and is set down at the right hand of the throne of God.

Psalm 37:23
The steps of a good man are ordered by the Lord, and he delightest in his way.

Isaiah 40 31
But they that wait upon the Lord shall renew their strength; they shall mount up with wings like eagles; they shall run, and not be weary; and they shall walk, and not faint.

Romans 1:10
Making request, if by any means now at length I might have a prosperous journey by the will of God to come unto you.

Philippians 2:16
Holding forth the word of life, that I may rejoice in the day of Christ that I have not run in vain, neither labored in vain.

Philippians: 3:14
I press toward the mark for the prize of the high calling of God in Christ Jesus.

Thirsty

Fancy clothes, fine jewelry
Shiny brass, diamond rings
And all these things…
Not enough…
Just won't measure up

Riches of silver…
Luxuries of gold
Power and wealth,
Riches untold…
Not enough…
Just won't measure up

Fame and Fortune,
Worldly treasures
Love of money,
Love of Pleasure
Not enough…
Just won't measure up

Unlimited Power
Unlimited Success
No time or
room to find happiness
Not enough…
Just won't measure up

After all the riches,
After all the fame

And empty vessel
Still yet remains

The power of God's Love
is priceless
Means more than
anything

Nothing on earth
can measure
The comfort and joy
He brings

These worldly things are
Not enough…
Just won't measure up…

My soul is thirsty Lord
Please…

Fill My Empty Cup!

Thirsty

Matthew 5: 6
Blessed are they which do hunger and thirst after righteousness: for they shall be filled.

John 4:14
But whosoever drinketh of the water that I shall give him shall never thirst; but the water that I shall give him shall be in him a well of water springing up into everlasting life.

John 7:37
If any man thirst let him come unto me, and drink.

Revelation 7:16
They shall hunger no more, neither thirst any more; neither shall the sun light on them, nor any heat.

Philippians 4:19
But my God shall supply all your need according to his riches in glory by Christ Jesus.

Matthew 6:21-22
For where your treasure is, there will your heart be also.
The lamp of the body is the eye; if, therefore, thine eye be healthy, thy whole body shall be full of light.

2

Seeking God's Guidance
"Follow Jesus"

I am the light of the world: he that followeth me shall not walk in darkness, but shall have the light of life.

John 8:12 KJV

A Prayer for Guidance

O Lord, I am striving to be a faithful and humble servant. When the way seems dark…help me to understand that You will never leave me alone. Your light will guide and show the path You have set for me to follow. I pray for strength to be faithful and dedicated to serve and follow You always with Gladness, Gratefulness and Humility in my Heart.

Amen

The Path

Sometimes I wonder
Where I am going
I drift along
From here to there

Not really knowing
My sense of purpose
What can I offer
What can I share

I search for answers
Sometimes alone
Inspiration
To find the dream

The path has many
Turns and directions…
Doors unopened
The road yet unseen

Searching and searching
Quest seems so futile
Sheltered thoughts
Masked by confusion

Where do I turn
Where do I go
This journey…it seems
A fictitious illusion

Why am I lost
Why can't I know
A tangled web
So confining…

Which way is right
Which way is left
Dreams hopeful
Still yet binding…

Realizing the path
Of my inner desires
And unconquered
Aspirations

Lies solely upon the
Promises of God…
With Him…just possibilities
No limitations

For God is
The way…The truth
And the Light…
He will provide
A clear path to make…

The pathway brighter
The road much clearer…
Rugged plains…
He will make straight

I must trust in Him
With my whole heart
Learn to be patient
Each and everyday…

Follow in His footsteps…
Let Him guide my Path…

For Here I am Lord
…Lead the Way!!!

The Path

John 12:26 NIV
Whoever serves me must follow me; and where I am, my servant also will be. My Father will honor the one who serves me.

Matthew 16:24
If any may will come after me, let him deny himself, and take up his cross, and follow me.

1Peter 2:21
For even hereunto were ye called; because Christ also suffered for us, leaving us an example, that ye should follow his steps.

Matthew 16:24-25NIV
If anyone would come after me, he must deny himself and take up his cross and follow me. For whoever wants to save his life will lose it, but whoever loses his life for me will find it.

Psalm: 119:105
Thy word is a lamp to my feet, and a light unto my path.

Isaiah 30:21NIV
Whether you turn to the right or to the left, your ears will hear a voice behind you saying, "This is the way; walk in it."

Proverbs 4:11NIV
I guide you in the way of wisdom and lead you along straight paths.

Psalm 16:11
Thou wilt show me the path of life: In thy presence is fullness of joy; at thy right hand there are pleasures for evermore.

2 Samuel 22:29 NIV
You are my lamp, O Lord; the Lord turns my darkness into light.

Proverbs 3:5-6
Trust in the Lord with all thine heart and lean not unto thine own understanding. In all thy ways acknowledge him, and he shall direct thy paths.

Too Busy

Hey, Slow down
Where are you going…
Running around
Spinning your wheels

In a hurry
Going No where fast
Too Busy
Too Busy For Real

Too busy to laugh
Too busy to cry
Too busy to find the time

For important things
That life brings

In a hurry…
As life passes
You by…

Too Busy

Galatians 5:22 NIV
But the fruit of the spirit is love, joy, peace, patience, kindness, goodness, faithfulness, gentleness and self-control.

Psalm 46:10
Be still, and know that I am God.

Philippians 4-6
Be anxious for nothing, but in everything, by prayer and supplication with thanksgiving, let your requests be made known unto God.

Isaiah 40:31
But they that wait upon the Lord shall renew their strength; they shall mount up with wings like eagles; they shall run, and not be weary; and they shall walk, and not faint.

Luke 21:19 NIV
By standing firm you will gain life.

If I Could...

If I could...I would ask Lord
Please grant me this...

How to walk upright with humility
In love and righteousness

If I could, I would ask for
wisdom and the strength of courage and
Not fear...to find

Trust and believe...
You have not given us the spirit of fear
But that of power, love and of a sound mind

If I could...I would ask for patience
To learn to trust You with my whole heart
And my soul...

Lean not to my own understanding
And in all thy ways acknowledge You...
And believe with assurance
You are in control

If I could...I would ask for tolerance
And thoughtfulness
To care

For the concern and
Well-being of others
Who may be lost in a sea of despair

If I could…I would reach out and touch
Each raindrop and
Create in it a song…

Water my soul with joyous melodies
To praise Your name
All the day long

If I could…I would light a candle
Of thankfulness within my heart
To shine over
And over again

If I could…I would ask these things…
And believe…All things are possible…

Because with You God…

I CAN!!!

If I Could...

Mark 10:27
With men it is impossible, but not with God; for with God all things are possible.

Mark 9:23
If thou believe, all things are possible to him that believeth.

Philippians 2:4NIV
Each of you should look not only to your own interests, but also to the interests of others.

2 Timothy 1:7-8
For God has not given us a spirit of fear; but of power, and of love, and of a sound mind.

Psalm 27:1
The Lord is my light and my salvation; whom shall I fear? The Lord is the strength of my life; of whom shall I be afraid?

Beatitudes Of a Christian Marriage

Blessed are the parents who find wisdom in the word of God day by day
Building a unity of love, commitment and respect as they go about their way

Blessed are the meek who love and give it unselfishly…
Sometimes having almost nothing, yet rely on God to truly make a way unconditionally

Blessed are the parents who meditate and pray
Seeking God's guidance to protect their children, least they go astray

Blessed is the woman with whom God has truly blessed
To be a wife, mother, counselor and friend…For with God as her strength and shield, she is able to stand any test

Blessed is the Godly man…for with him a daily walk with God is taken
The strength of his way is found in his kindness and deeds. But his love of the Lord is never shaken

Blessed are they who are loved and give love
For God…is love!

Blessed are they who build their house on a solid foundation
For their house will be grounded on God's Holy Word! The solid rock Of our salvation!

Blessed are they that laugh together, love together, and pray together
For theirs is the tie that bind

Blessed are they who have chosen to walk with God…
For the Lord shall renew their strength, they shall mount up with wings as eagles, they shall run and not be weary, and they shall walk and not faint

Blessed…be the name of the Lord.

Beatitudes
Of a Christian Marriage

Matthew 5:7
Blessed are the merciful: for they shall obtain mercy.

1 Peter 1:22 NIV
Love one another deeply, from the heart.

Psalm 128:1
Blessed is every one that feareth the Lord, that walketh in his ways.

Psalm 128:3-4
Thy wife shall be as a fruitful vine by the sides of thine house; thy children like olive plants round about thy table. Behold, that thus shall the man be blessed who feareth the Lord.

Proverbs 31:10
Who can find a virtuous woman? For her price is far above rubies.

Proverbs 31:25
Strength and honor are her clothing, and she shall rejoice in time to come.

Proverbs 31:26 NIV
She speaks with wisdom, and faithful instruction is on her tongue.

Ephesians 5:31
For this cause shall a man leave his father and mother, and shall be joined unto his wife, and they shall be one flesh.

1 Corinthians 6:17
But he that is joined unto the Lord is one spirit.

Forgive Me

In the morning
With the rising of the sun
I ask Lord…
What have I done

Again, I have fallen
From Your grace
Another sorrow
I can't erase

Temptation veers
On every hand
Now I have fallen
Once again

I'm not worthy
Of Your Holy Will
In spite of my faults
You care for me…
You love me…still

Forgive Me…

Forgive Me

Matthew 6:14
For if ye forgive men their trespasses, your heavenly father will also forgive you.

Psalm 86:3
Be merciful unto me, O Lord: for I cry unto thee daily.

Psalm 86:5
For thou, Lord, art good, and ready to forgive, and plenteous in mercy unto all those who call upon thee.

2 Corinthians: 2:10
To whom ye forgive anything, I forgive also: for if I forgave anything, to whom I forgave it, for your sakes forgave I it in the person of Christ.

1 John 1:9
If we confess our sins, he is faithful and just to forgive us our sins, and to cleanse us from all unrighteousness.

Ephesians 4:32
And be ye kind one to another, tenderhearted, forgiving one another, even as God for Christ's sake hath forgiven you.

3

Proclaiming The Joy!

I will praise you, O Lord, with all my heart; I will tell of all Your wonders. I will be glad and rejoice in you; I will sing praise to your name, O Most High.

            Psalm 9:1-2 NIV

A Prayer Of Joyfulness

Lord, You are the Joy and Strength of my life.
I will praise Your Name because You are Great and Greatly to be Praised. I pray that Your loving and ever present grace abide within my heart always so that I may rejoice and proclaim Your goodness to give You all the glory and honor due Your Holy and Righteous Name.

Amen

I get Joy

When I think about
His goodness
And what He's done for me

I get Joy

Just praising His name
Over and over
Continuously

I get Joy

In the morning…
In the evening…
And all the day long

I get Joy

For in my heart
He has given me
A song

I get Joy

Proclaiming His goodness
Knowing He is Lord of Lord and
Kings of Kings

I get Joy

For He is my
All and All
He is
My Everything

I Get Joy

Philippians 4:4
Rejoice in the Lord always; and again I say, Rejoice.

Proverbs 15:30 NIV
A cheerful look brings joy to the heart, and good news gives health to the bones.

Matthew 5:12
Rejoice, and be exceeding glad: for great is your reward in heaven.

Psalm 34:1
I will bless the Lord at all times: his praise shall continually be in my mouth.

1 Thessalonians 5:16-18
Rejoice evermore. Pray without ceasing. In everything give thanks: for this is the will of God in Christ Jesus concerning you.

John 15:11
These things have I spoken unto you, that my joy might remain in you, and that your joy might be full.

Psalm 100:1-2 NIV
Shout for joy to the Lord, all the earth. Worship the Lord with gladness; come before him with joyful songs.

Psalm 32:11
Be glad in the Lord, and rejoice, ye righteous: and shout for joy, all ye that are upright in heart.

Psalm 34:3
O magnify the Lord with me, and let us exalt his name together.

A Song Bird Chorus

Early in the morning at the
break of dawn…
A chorus of songbirds begin
To sing their song

Their melodies sweep the
atmosphere
With a chant so reverent
and free

A rendition of songs
to glorify…
His Holy Name
in
perfect harmony

Their clocks are posed
to rise with hope
Their wings set on coarse
with a mission

A chorus of little
Song Birds…
singing their song…
A Joyous Praise
I love to listen

A melody so sweet
and harmonious
In so many
wonderful ways

Oh Little Song Birds…
Sing loud, Sing happy
For you are
An Instrument of Praise

In the still of the day
A chant remains clear
Ever lingering
To sustain

A Fellowship of Praise
From little Song Birds
Rejoicing and Lifting
His Holy Name

So catch a tune
In your heart
Sing and Rejoice
in it always

Like the Songbirds Sing
Let your Praises Ring…

With a Song and
A Melody of
Praise!

A Song Bird Chorus

Psalm 66:1-2
Make a joyful noise unto God, all ye lands: Sing forth the honour of his name: make his praise glorious.

Psalm 97:1
The Lord reigneth; let the earth rejoice; let the multitude of isles be glad thereof.

Ephesians 5:19
Speaking to yourselves in psalms and hymns and spiritual songs, singing and making melody in your heart to the Lord.

Psalm 66:4
All the earth shall worship thee, and shall sing unto thee; they shall sing to thy name. Selah.

Psalm 9:2
I will be glad and rejoice in thee: I will sing praise to thy name, O thou most High.

Psalm 33: 1
Rejoice in the Lord, O ye righteous: for praise is comely for the upright.

Psalm 47:6
Sing praises to God, sing praises: sing praises unto our King, sing praises.

Psalm 98:4
Make a joyful noise unto the Lord, all the earth; make a loud noise, and rejoice, and sing praise.

Psalm 100:1-2
Make a joyful noise unto the Lord, all ye lands. Serve the Lord with gladness: come before his presence with singing.

By The Window

A moment of reflection
Looking out my window
Into the silent and
still of night

Sitting ever so still
Capturing the view
Of a majestic wonder of lights

Wandering thoughts
Begin to linger
Beholding a starry creation

In awe of His goodness,
His mighty works
My heart is
Overjoyed with elation

A whispering breeze awaken
The silence of the night...
I sit, I think, and I Ponder

By the window
A view and sequence of beauty
His power, and might
What an awesome wonder

A moment
Contemplating thoughts
A moment lost in time

A moment to hope
A moment to dream
A moment of inspiration to find

By the window I sit
Inhibitions sustained
A clear view now in sight

By the window I sit
A once weary mind restored
Possibilities endless
With God…
As a Guiding light

By The Window

Psalm 118:23-24
This is the Lord's doing; it is marvellous in our eyes. This is the day which the Lord hath made; we will rejoice and be glad in it.

Matthew 19:26
But Jesus beheld them, and said unto them, with men this is impossible; but with God all things are possible.

Psalm 8:3
When I consider thy heavens, the work of thy fingers, the moon and the stars, which thou hast ordained.

Luke 1:37
For with God nothing shall be impossible.

Colors of love

A symbol of Peace
A Promise that binds
A covenant to remember
His love ever shines

Lighting the sky
Colors of Love
Luster of beauty
Reign down from above

The light of Heaven
Painting the Sky
A band of true colors
His love we can't deny

A joy to behold
A moment in time
A lasting Promise
Of God's Love
So Divine…

Colors of Love

Acts 3:25
Ye are the children of the prophets, and of the covenant which God made with our fathers, saying unto Abraham, AND IN THY SEED SHALL ALL THE KINDREDS OF THE EARTH BE BLESSED.

Genesis 9:12-16 NIV
And God said, "This is the sign of the covenant I am making between me and you and every living creature with you, a covenant for all generations to come: I have set my rainbow in the clouds, and it will be the sign of the covenant between me and the earth. Whenever I bring clouds over the earth and the rainbow appears in the clouds, I will remember my covenant between me and you and all living creatures of every kind.

Formula III

No, it's not a pain
Reliever, supplement
Medication or pill

No, it's not a sedative
For aches and pain or
A prescription to refill

No, it doesn't come in
A bottle…A quick
Remedy to fix

No, it's not sold
Over the counter…
In a bottled drink
Or Mix

No, it can not
Be returned
With a money
Back guarantee

No, it's not a bargain…
Buy One…
Get One Free…

No, it doesn't have
Fine tiny print
Written
On it's label
For directions

No, it's not designed
To hide, camouflage
Or conceal imperfections

No special card
Or instructions
Are needed
For this formula
To purchase or buy

Just present your request
In faith…through prayer
To the Almighty Father
On High

He knows and prepares
The right dosage
For our desires
And our needs

Each request
He will gladly fill…
If we only trust Him
And just believe

A daily dose work
Wonders for the
Sin sick soul

When depression weighs
You down…it lifts you up…
And help you to make it
When the world and life
Seems so cold

Every ounce is measured
And filled with love
And care

Each dose will yield
Bountiful blessings…
Overflowing…
Enough to share

It is available
Not in a bottle
But only thru His grace

Taking it daily
Will provide
Strength and determination
To run this Christian race

This formula is good
For the body, the mind
And the soul

Taken daily, it can
Restore, regenerate
And make you
Completely whole

Take Formula III
Each and everyday
In a healthy dose

For best results
Take as directed

One for the Father…
One for the Son…

And one for the
Holy Ghost…

God is so good
O taste and see

For relief of aches and pain
Take a generous dose
of
Formula III

Formula III

Psalm 42:11
Why art thou cast down, O my soul? And why art thou disquieted within me? Hope thou in God; for I shall yet praise him, who is the health of my countenance, and my God.

Isaiah 53:5
But he was wounded for our transgressions, he was bruised for our iniquities: the chastisement of our peace was upon him; and with his stripes we are healed.

Romans 8:26-27 NIV
In the same way, the Spirit helps us in our weakness. We do not know what we ought to pray for, but the Spirit himself intercedes for us with groans that words cannot express. And he who searches our hearts knows the mind of the Spirit, because the Spirit intercedes for the saints in accordance with God's will.

Ephesians 4:3-6
Endeavoring to keep the unity of the spirit in the bond of peace. There is one body, and one spirit, even as ye are called in one hope of your calling; One Lord, one Faith, one Baptism, One God and Father of all who is above all, and through all, and in you all.

2 Corinthians 12:9
And he said unto me, My grace is sufficient for thee: for my strength is made perfect in weakness.

Psalm 34:8
O taste and see that the Lord is good; blessed is the man who trusteth in him.

John 4:24
God is a spirit; and they that worship him must worship him in spirit and in truth.

Exodus 15:11
Who is like unto thee, O Lord, among the Gods? Who is like thee, glorious in holiness, fearful in praises, doing wonders?

Jeremiah 10:10
But the Lord is the true God; he is the living God, and an everlasting King; at his wrath the earth shall tremble, and the nations shall not be able to abide his indignation.

Jeremiah 33:6
Behold, I will bring it health and cure, and I will cure them, and will reveal unto them the abundance of peace and truth.

4

Deliverance

"Words of Encouragement"

God is our refuge and strength, a
very present help in trouble.

Psalm 46:1 KJV

A Prayer of Deliverance

Oh Lord, keep me in Your care and sanctify my heart to do Your Holy Will each and everyday. In times of trouble, help me look to the hills from whence cometh my help, knowing that my help cometh from You.
Teach me to faithfully grow in Your Word so that
I may always seek You first in
all that I do.

Amen

Be of Good Courage...

Why bury your head in the sand...
For what can you see?

Inside the darkness
There lies no light...
Just sorrow, grief and misery

Be of good courage
For strength comes from within

This race isn't given
To the swift
Nor victory to the strong...

But to those who
Endureth
To the end.

Be of Good Courage

Romans 8:25NIV
But if we hope for what we do not yet have, we wait for it patiently.

John 16:33
These things I have spoken unto you, that in me ye might have peace. In the world ye shall have tribulation; but be of good cheer; I have overcome the world.

Lamentations 3:25-26 NIV
The Lord is good to those whose hope is in him, to the one who seeks him; it is good to wait quietly for the salvation of the Lord.

Psalm 27:14
Wait on the Lord: be of good courage, and he shall strengthen thine heart: wait, I say on the Lord.

A Spider's Song

The day dawns with a break of light
A task in hand for a spider's delight

Making a home to dwell and entangle within
Much like the castle of a lion's den

Round and round, the spider composes
A melody of lines, like a sweet bouquet of roses

In harmony, the sound is sweet, and in tune
A vision of beauty and elegance, its web
Will unveil soon

For how does it know the seeming ingredient
How does it know the necessary skill

It knows what it know…
For it has instilled…a given talent
And knowledge, only God can reveal

Knowing though the home of silk may soon
Fall to unsuspecting prey

What a wonderful thing to see how nature
Sings its song in such a beautiful way

A little spider in a big world it seems
Finds no intimidation

For it meets its challenge with "skill and love"
What a winning combination

For just like the spider's web
Our song too can be heard…

And the joy is that the beauty of our song
Can be seen…

In our actions, our thoughts, and
Our words

A Spider's Song

Psalm 84:4
Blessed are they that dwell in thy house; they will be still praising thee. Selah.

Jeremiah 10:6
Forasmuch as there is none like unto thee, O Lord; thou art great, and thy name is great in might.

2 Corinthians 9:11
Being enriched in everything to all bountifulness, which causeth through us thanksgiving to God.

2 Timothy 1:6
Wherefore I put thee in remembrance that thou stir up the gift of God, which is in thee by the putting on of my hands.

James 1:17
Every good gift and every perfect gift is from above, and cometh down from the Father of lights, with whom is no variableness, neither shadow of turning.

2 Corinthians 9:15
Thanks be unto God for his unspeakable gift.

Why

Someone may ask
Why do I dream
And imagine things that could be

Why build my hopes to right a wrong…
Just to try and save
humanity

Someone may wonder…
why sacrifice
For I am only one

For without a dream…
there is no vision
No race to ever be won

Someone may ask
why do I smile
After all my pain gets
hard to bear

But if you look beyond
my tears
Inside my heart…
The joy of His love
Dwells there

Sometime I ask the
question
Lord, Why?
It seems trouble is present
on every hand

But deep within He gives
Me strength
He is my closest friend…

For He lets me know
The question is not to ask
Or wonder why the test…

Just have faith…
Do the right thing…
Be willing to do your best

And if you wonder
Why I believe in my heart
I can dream

I know that God in us is love…
And with Him…
We can do anything…

Why

Psalm 37:23
The steps of a good man are ordered by the Lord: and he delighteth in his way.

Psalm 139:23
Search me, O God, and know my heart: try me, and know my thoughts.

Philippians 3:14
I press toward the mark for the prize of the high calling of God in Christ Jesus.

Matthew 19:26
But Jesus beheld them, and said unto them, with men this is impossible; but with God all things are possible.

Luke 1:37
For with God nothing shall be impossible.

Available

To be loving
Faithful
Kindhearted and true

To be sincere
Patient
In all that I do

To serve You
With gladness
My heart to renew

Lord, I'm willing
I'm Yours

And I'm
Available to You!

Available

Philippians 1:6
Being confident of this very thing, that he which hath begun a good work in you will perform it until the day of Jesus Christ.

Philippians 1:24-25
Nevertheless to abide in the flesh is more needful for you.
And having this confidence, I know that I shall abide and continue with you all for your furtherance and joy of faith.

Philippians 2:13
For it is God which worketh in you both to will and to do of his good pleasure.

Philippians 3:14
I press toward the mark for the prize of the high calling of God in Christ Jesus.

Philippians 4:13
I can do all things through Christ which strengthens me.

The Challenge

Life is a journey…
Challenges may arise

Long still to press forward…
Keep your eyes on the prize

Live to learn…learn to live
Your dreams to fulfill

Listen always to your heart…
Run on with patience
And a determined will

Let no unexpected obstacle
Obstruct or deter your plans

Lean not to your own
Understanding

Keep your hands
In God's Hands

Look to the hills from
Whence cometh
Your help…

Believe…Seek Confidence
And assurance…

But most of all…

Challenge Yourself

The Challenge

Matthew 6:33
But seek ye first the kingdom of God, and his righteousness; and all these things shall be added unto you

Philippians 4:13
I can do all things through Christ which strengtheneth me.

Psalm 85:13
Righteousness shall go before him; and shall set us in the way of his steps.

Mark 5:37
Be not afraid, only believe

2 Corinthians 8:12 NIV
For if the willingness is there, the gift is acceptable according to what one has, not according to what he does not have.

Philippians 3:14
I press toward the mark for the prize of the high calling of God in Christ Jesus.

Symphony

It is Sweet
It is Complete
Like music to my ears...

It is Pure...
It is Sincere
A sound so joyous to hear

It is soothing
It is touching
Gives me harmony
And peace inside

It is Poetry
It is a song
Rings gloriously
With pride

It is happiness
It is angelic
Flows so graciously

It is satisfying
It is gratifying
A resounding chord
Of virtuosity

A beautiful Inspiration
To listen and hear
Composed so wonderfully
Ever so dear

A glorious melody
Fulfilling and sweet
The Name of Jesus…

A Symphony…
Complete!!!

Symphony

Psalm 8:9
O Lord our Lord, how excellent is thy name in all the earth!

Psalm 83:18
That men may know that thou, whose name alone is the Lord, art the Most High over all the

Psalm 72:17
His name shall endure forever; his name shall be continued as long as the sun, and men shall be blessed in him: All nations shall call him blessed.

1 Chronicles 29:13
Now therefore, our God, we thank thee, and praise thy glorious name.

Psalm 72:19
And blessed be his glorious name forever: and let the whole earth be filled with his glory; Amen, and Amen.

Stand

Believe with conviction
Find justice within
Be mindful of truth
For victory to win

When others lose hope
And doubt your intentions
Stand up for right
Your heart, God will strengthen

Follow your belief
And conscious inside
Speak bold with humility
Courageous, yet wise

Believe in yourself
Stand firm, despite
Odds…

Stand with strength
Stand with courage

But most of all…

Stand Still…
And know that I am

God

Stand

Psalm 45:4
And in thy majesty ride prosperously because of truth and meekness and righteousness; and thy right hand shall teach thee awe-inspiring things.

Psalm 85:13
Righteousness shall go before him, and shall set us in the way of his steps.

Exodus 14:14
The Lord shall fight for you, and ye shall hold your peace.

Isaiah 40:29
He giveth power to the faint; and to them that have no might he increaseth strength.

Psalm 27:1
The Lord is my light and my salvation; whom shall I fear? The Lord is the strength of my life; of whom shall I be afraid?

Psalm 19: 14
Let the words of my mouth, and the meditation of my heart, be acceptable in thy sight, O Lord, my strength and my redeemer.

1 Chronicles 28:20 NIV
Be strong and courageous, and do the work. Do not be afraid or discouraged, for the Lord God, my God is with you.

Psalm 46:10
Be still, and know that I am God.

Joshua 1:19 NIV
Be strong and courageous. Do not be terrified; do not be discouraged, for the Lord your God will be with you wherever you go.

James 1:2-3NIV
Consider it pure joy, my brothers, whenever you face trials of many kinds, because you know that the testing of your faith develops perseverance.

Psalm 84:12
For the Lord God is a sun and shield; the Lord will give grace and glory. No good thing will he withhold from them that walk upright.

The Divine Creator Awe ~Inspiring

Oh God, My God…
How Awe~ Inspiring…
The Wonder of
Your Marvelous Works

A Vision Inspired…
Uniquely engrained
Upon the embodiment
of the Universe

A miraculous plan…
A Genesis conceived
Formed and Created upon
Command

A palette of Beauty…
Divinely revealed
By the works of Your
Wondrous Hands

Oh God, My God…
How awesome You are
Like an Artist with an
empty slate

You formed…
You shaped…You fashioned
A Masterpiece to
Create

In the beginning…
as it is written…God Created…
And the Heavens and the

Earth became
known

Where there was
nothing….
God conceived and
designed a world
All His
Own

With the emptiness
of darkness all around
and in the silent and
still of night…

He Awakened the
Heavens with a fiery ball
And then God said…
Let there be Light

And the light
He called day
And the darkness night…
And He saw that
it was Good…A Wondrous and
Marvelous Sight

And the earth brought forth
an abundance
The grass, the herb…
the fruit and
Creatures after
his kind

The Heavens Reveled
in its Glory Beaming Lights

of the Sun, Moon and the
Stars to reign above
To Forever Shine

And all that was
Created
He saw that it was
Good…
Yet He Envisioned
Still a Plan

To Form in His own
Image and Likeness
The
Creation of Man

Like a Potter
Sculpting Clay…
In His Hands, He did Mold…

The Shape and Essence
of our Being
Our mind…Our body…
and
Our Soul

And He looked and
Saw that Everything
He Had Created
Was Good and on the
Seventh day rested
and Blessed
His Creation

For His mighty
Works are Great

And will Stand Firm
Forever throughout
All Generations

Oh God, My God…
How Awe ~Inspiring
Your Creative
Spirit and Works
So Divine

For You have Instilled
Within Us
A Gifted Spirit…
Our Purpose and
Destiny to Find

We are Fruits of Your Labor
Fearfully and
Wonderfully Made
By Your Almighty and
Powerful Hands

Inspired of Your Imagination
All Part of a
Divine
Master Plan

For Everything That is…
And That Which is
Everything…
Every Creature…
Every Shape…Every Form

You Envisioned
a Creation of Life

And of Life…
a Creation was Born

Oh God, My God…
You are the
Source of my Life
And the Light
of my
Inspiration…
For You Painted a
Portrait
For the Whole World
To See…

A Vision…
A Living Portrait
You Painted it all…
Just For You
and Me…

Oh God, My God
How Awe-Inspiring…
For You are the
Generator…
The Innovator
and the
Creator of my
Soul…

God, our Father…
Your Mighty Works…

So Amazing…
to
Behold!

The Divine Creator
Awe–Inspiring

Psalm 40:5
Many, O lord; my God are thy wonderful works which thou hast done, and thy thoughts which are towards us; they cannot be reckoned up in order unto thee. If I would declare and speak of them, they are more than can be numbered.

Isaiah 45:12
I have made the earth, and created man upon it; I even my hands, have stretched out the heaven, and all their host I commanded.

Psalm 145:5-6 NIV
They will speak of the glorious splendor of your majesty, and I will meditate on your wonderful works. They will tell of the power of your awesome works, and I will proclaim your great deeds.

Revelation 15:3
And thy sing the song of Moses, the servant of God, and the song of the lamb, saying, great and marvelous are thy works, Lord God Almighty; just and true are thy ways, thou King of Saints.

Psalm 92:4
For thou, Lord hast made me glad through thy work; I will triumph in the works of thy hands.

Psalm 92:5
O Lord, how great are thy works! And thy thoughts are very deep.

Psalm 90:17
And let the beauty of the Lord our God be upon us, and establish thou the work of Our hands upon us; yea, the work of our hands establish thou us.

Psalm 139:14
I will praise thee; for I am fearfully and wonderfully made. Marvelous are thy works, and that my soul knoweth right well.

Jeremiah 10:12
He hath made the earth by his power; he hath established the world by his wisdom, and hath stretched out the heavens by his understanding.

Deuteronomy 10:21
He is thy praise, and he is thy God, who hath done for thee these great and awe-inspiring things which thine eyes have see.

Psalm 99:3
Let them praise thy great and awe-inspiring name for it is holy.

Psalm 145:6
And men shall speak of the might of thy awe-inspiring acts; and I will declare thy greatness.

Psalm 86:10
For thou art great, and doest wondrous things; thou art God alone..

Psalm 118:23
This is the Lord's doing; it is marvelous in our eyes.

Psalm 33:6
By the word of the Lord were the heavens made; and all the host of them by the breath of his mouth.

5

A Prayer For All Seasons

Prayer for Daily Guidance

O, Lord, we are in daily need of Your protection each and everyday. Give us grace and compassion to be just and upright in all of our daily deeds. Lead and guide, keeping us always under Your wings of protection.
In Christ Jesus name we pray.

Amen

Prayer for Dedication of Soul and Body

O gracious Father, we hereby dedicate our souls and our bodies to do Your Holy Will. Confirm and strengthen us, that we may grow in wisdom and grace.

Amen

Prayer for Christian Service

O Lord, our Heavenly Father, strengthen those in the ministry of service with wisdom, patience and courage to minister to those in need. Guide the way for the anointed to teach in a spiritual, loving and most righteous way, keeping Your Word as a guiding light for all to see.

Amen

Prayer for The Children

O Lord, protect and guide the children that they may be strengthened by Your goodness and mercy to grow stronger each and everyday. Give them grace to be obedient to Your Holy Word. Lead, guide, and keep them forever present in your care.

Amen

A General Prayer Of Thanksgiving

Almighty God, we do give most humble thanks for all Your goodness and loving kindness. For Your wondrous creation and blessings of life we thank You. Enlighten our hearts, that we may be infinitely thankful to give You all the praise and the glory.

Amen

A Prayer for the Missions

O Lord, we pray for those who minister to those in communities all around the world. We pray that You will bless them to minister the word of hope, peace and love, to share the goodness of Your grace to all in need of prayer and a blessing.

Amen

A Prayer for Fruitful Seasons

Almighty God, bless the earth to be bountiful and fruitful and to bring forth the reap of harvest upon the land we pray. Bless the labourers who harvest the fields, and grant, seasonable weather that we may gather the fruits of the earth, and rejoice in the goodness of Your blessings each and everyday.

Amen

A Prayer for Memorial Days

Almighty God, our Heavenly Father, we give thanks for all those who have laid down their lives for the service of our country. We pray that their works will be a remembrance of unselfish labor. Let their hearts be sustained in knowing that through their good works and deed the comfort of Your grace and mercy will be ever-present always.

Amen

A Prayer for the Clergy and People

Almighty and everlasting God, we pray for Your blessings and spiritual guidance upon ministers, clergy and upon the congregation to be committed to their charge in efforts to do Your Holy Will. May the spirit of Your grace guide those to serve and praise Your Holy Name with gladness forever and ever.

Amen

A Prayer for Those under affliction

O Merciful God, we pray that You would look upon the sorrows of your servant for whom our prayers are offered. Remember him, O Lord in mercy, and endow his soul with patience. Comfort and strengthen him daily with Your mercy and grace.

Amen

A Prayer in time Of Famine

O God, our Heavenly Father, who has given us the gift of abundance…in the rain that falls and the bountiful harvest of the earth. Restore unto us in time of need, nourishment for our bodies and replenish, O Lord, the fruits of the earth for the relief of the suffering and of mankind. Prayerfully, we ask in Jesus Christ, our Lord and Saviour's Name.

Amen

A Prayer for Families

Almighty and everlasting God, watch over us day by day. Protect, guide, and keep the bond of family unity together to grow stronger with Your guidance always.

Amen

Personal Prayer

Inspirational Quote

"How can you say what you feel? How can you write what's in your heart? How can you find the words...when there are no words?...Only through His Goodness... His Direction...His Leadership and His Guidance... The Writer and the Creator of my Inspiration. Only God!!!

Doris M. Batson

About the Authors

Doris M. Batson, writing poetry of hope and compassion are the messages she inspires to write. Her work is refreshingly uplifting to all who seek a desire to find the inner fulfillment and discovery of Joy. Aside from being a prolific writer of inspirational poetry, she is also a musician and an arts educator as well. She has one daughter, Brittany DeVonne Batson, and resides currently in her hometown of Tyler, Texas.

    Rev. P.R. Moore, currently serves as pastor of the Mt. Sinai Missionary Baptist Church in Big Sandy, Texas. As a pastor and minister, his inspiration and passion dwells in studying, teaching and ministering the word of the gospel. Although this book is his first published work, he has written many unpublished writings of sermons, prayers, and poetry as well. He is married and has three children, three grandchildren, and one great grandchild.

    To contact the authors, or if you would like to receive a copy of this book, you may write to:

Doris M. Batson, or
Rev. P.R. Moore
P.O. Box 1331
Lindale, Texas 75771

0-595-33903-4

Printed in the United States
30002LVS00005B/313-375